W9-BRA-953

ANCIENT CIVILIZATIONS

Egypt

By Christy Steele

Steadwell
Books

Raintree Steck-Vaughn Publishers
A Harcourt Company

Austin · New York
www.steck-vaughn.com

67.220

Published by Raintree Steck-Vaughn Publishers, an imprint of Steck-Vaughn Company.

Library of Congress Cataloging-in-Publication Data
Cataloging-in-Publication data is available upon request.

Produced by Compass Books

Photo Acknowledgments
Corbis/Richard T. Nowitz, 10; Gianni Dagli Orti, 17, 25; Roger Wood, 20, 38;
    Charles & Josette Lenars, 22; Archivo Iconografico, 33; Bettmann, 37
Photo Network, cover; Paul Thompson, title page; Wolf, 12; Ahmad M.
Abdalla, 30
Root Resources/Claudia Adams, 14, 26
Visuals Unlimited, 18; Max & Bea Hunn, 29; Les Christman, 34; Inga Spence,
    40, 47; Charles Sanders, 42

Content Consultant
Dr. Melinda K. Hartwig
Institute of Egyptian Art and Archaeology
Memphis, Tennessee

Don L. Curry
Educational Author, Editor, Consultant, and Columnist

J932
STV

Contents

These three pyramids at Giza are the largest pyramids in Egypt.

About Egypt

In about 3100 B.C., the Egyptian **civilization** started along the Nile River in Africa. A civilization is an advanced society. A society shares a common way of life. Egypt was the longest lasting civilization of the ancient world. Ancient means old.

Egyptian people built large cities, **pyramids**, **temples**, and statues. Pyramids were huge tombs built for kings. A tomb is a place where someone is buried. A temple is a building used for worshiping gods. The remains of some ancient Egyptian tombs, temples, and cities still stand today.

Where Was the Egyptian Civilization?

The Egyptian civilization grew on the land around the Nile from the Mediterranean Sea down to the top of Nubia. Nubia was the country south of Egypt. The Egyptians also took over several foreign places. Foreign means coming from another country.

Most of Egypt was desert. A desert is a dry area of land. Egyptian people built large cities near the Nile River. Land around the Nile had rich soil. People could grow crops there to feed people living in the cities.

Egypt and the World

Most Egyptians were farmers. They raised wheat, barley, and melons. They planted fruit trees and grew grapes in vineyards.

Other Egyptians were merchants. Merchants are people who sell goods. Merchants loaded ships with goods and sailed to faraway places. They sold or traded their goods with other people. In this way, Egyptians learned about life in other places.

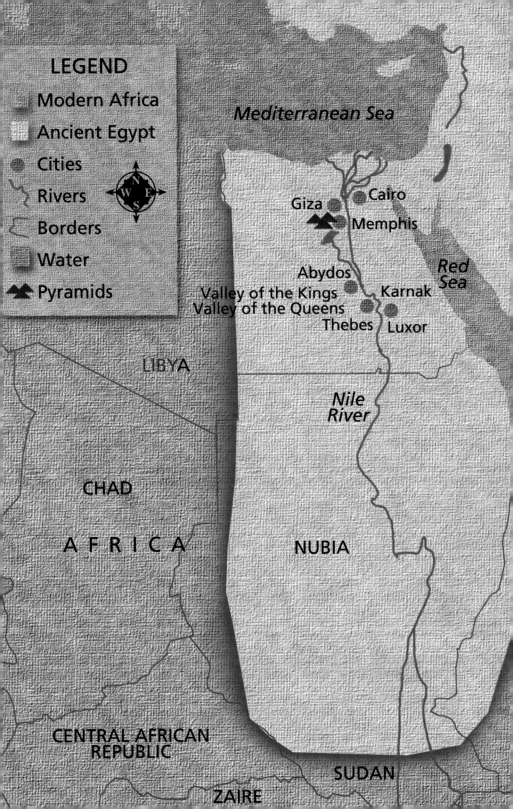

Egyptian History

At first, Egypt was made of two kingdoms, Upper Egypt and Lower Egypt. A kingdom is a place with a king or queen as its ruler. Around 3100 B.C., King Narmer of Upper Egypt took over Lower Egypt. He formed one government for all of Egypt.

Most of the history of ancient Egypt is broken into the Old, Middle, and New Kingdoms. Two Intermediate Periods separated the Kingdoms. Life was hard for Egyptians in the Intermediate Periods. Egyptians fought each other and people from other countries for power.

The Old Kingdom lasted from about 2750 to 2250 B.C. The first pyramids were built during the Old Kingdom.

The Middle Kingdom lasted from about 2025 to 1606 B.C. Egypt became powerful and traded with many peoples. Egyptian rulers built many large temples and more pyramids. They also took over parts of Nubia.

THE EGYPT TIMELINE

3100 B.C.	King Narmer unites Upper Egypt and Lower Egypt
2750 B.C. to 2250 B.C.	Old Kingdom
2250 B.C. to 2025 B.C.	First Intermediate Period
2025 B.C. to 1606 B.C.	Middle Kingdom
1606 B.C. to 1539 B.C.	Second Intermediate Period
1539 B.C. to 1070 B.C.	New Kingdom

The New Kingdom began in about 1539 B.C. and lasted until 1070 B.C. Egyptians began calling their rulers **pharaohs** during this time. Pharaohs fought wars in Asia and Nubia and took over more land.

 This painted carving shows a king watching farmers gather crops.

Egyptian Government

Thirty-one dynasties ruled ancient Egypt. A dynasty is a family or group that stays in power over many years. A king ruled each dynasty. Egyptian rulers were **god-kings**. People worshiped them. To worship is to honor and love someone or something as if it was a god. Rule over Egypt was usually passed down from a king to his oldest son.

Kings had the most power in Egypt. They forced Egyptians to work on large building projects, such as the pyramids. Kings could make Egypt go to war with other countries. They also kept part of everyone's yearly crops for themselves.

Kings needed help running Egypt. One or two men called **viziers** helped each king run Egypt. Many officials also helped. Kings split Egypt into parts called nomes. The king chose a person to be in charge of each nome. They were called governors. Governors collected taxes for the kings. They also enforced the laws of Egypt.

Priests were also important and powerful. They told Egyptians how to worship and please the gods. A high priest often acted for the king in worshiping and pleasing the gods.

This gold statue is of a young prince of Egypt. It was found in a tomb.

Life in Ancient Egypt

There were three **classes** of people in ancient Egypt. A class is a group of people who have similar jobs. There was no money in ancient Egypt. People were paid in goods and services.

The largest class was poor working people. They worked as servants, farmers, or shepherds. A shepherd raises and takes care of animals.

The middle class was made of merchants, soldiers, craftspeople, and **scribes**. Craftspeople made goods. Scribes were clerks, or writers.

The highest class was made of the king and ruling family and the families of the powerful. These families often had many servants working for them.

▲ This tomb painting shows Egyptian men wearing kilts.

What the Egyptians Wore

The weather in Egypt was very hot in summer. Egyptians wore simple clothes that helped them keep cool. Their clothes were made of a light, thin fabric called linen.

Egyptians sometimes wore **tunics**. A tunic is a straight, loose-fitting piece of clothing.

Tunics could have short sleeves or no sleeves. They could be different lengths. Young men wore knee-length tunics. Women and older men wore longer tunics.

Women sometimes wore straight, sleeveless dresses that came to their ankles. They wore short skirts if they were working. On special days, rich women wore fancy dresses decorated with beads and feathers.

Egyptian men also wore kilts. A kilt is fabric that is wrapped around the body like a skirt.

The clothing Egyptians wore changed slightly with the seasons. Men sometimes wore loincloths when they were working hard in the heat. A loincloth is a piece of cloth wrapped between the legs and around the waist. During winter, people often wore robes over their clothes.

Rich Egyptians wore jewelry to dress up their clothes. They wore necklaces, jeweled collars, bracelets, and earrings. They often put pictures of their gods on their jewelry.

Egyptian Homes

Egyptians built their houses on high ground to escape from Nile floods. They used dried mud-brick to build their homes. Houses had narrow doorways and small windows high in the walls. Woven mats covered the windows to keep out flies and desert sand. Roofs had several vents, or holes, that helped air move in and out of the houses. Roofs were flat. Families could sleep or cook on the roofs when the weather was hot.

Homes in the country often had a small courtyard in front. A courtyard is an open place surrounded by walls or buildings. A low mud-brick wall surrounded the courtyard. Families cooked in the courtyard. They sometimes kept a small pool of water there. They carried water in jugs from the river or nearby wells to keep the pool full.

Rich Egyptians had larger homes with large courtyards. The courtyards had large pools and gardens. The number of rooms and levels in the houses depended on how rich the

▲ This illustration shows what the inside of an Egyptian palace looked like.

family was. Rooms to greet and entertain guests were on the first floor. A hallway led into the rest of the house. The family lived in the back or the upper levels of the house. Colorful wall hangings and paintings were placed on the walls and ceilings. Tiles often covered the floors.

This ancient Egyptian painting shows farmers planting crops.

Food and Farming

Farming along the Nile was the center of life in Egypt. Every year, the Nile flooded. The floodwater left rich, dark soil called **silt** around the Nile's banks. The soil was good for growing crops.

Egyptian farmers learned how to **irrigate** their crops. To irrigate means to bring water to dry land. They dug canals from the Nile to their land. They dug deep holes called storage ditches along the canals. When the Nile flooded, it filled the canals and the storage ditches. The water stayed in the storage ditches when there was less water in the Nile. Throughout the year, farmers used water from the storage ditches to water their crops.

Barley was the main crop of the Egyptians. They used barley to make bread. They also grew fruit and vegetables, such as figs, dates, grapes, lettuce, cucumbers, and olives.

Egyptians also ate meat. They raised cattle, goats, and sheep. They also hunted animals, such as gazelle and birds. A gazelle is a deer-like animal. Fish was an important food. Egyptians caught and ate fish from the Nile.

This group of statues shows a king between two Egyptian goddesses.

Egyptian Culture

A group of people's ideas, customs, traditions, and way of life make up their **culture**. Egyptian people expressed their culture through the things they did and the things they made.

The Egyptians built temples and statues of their gods. This shows the importance of religion to Egyptian culture. Religion is belief and worship in a god or gods. Egyptian people also believed in life after death. They believed people went to the afterlife after they died. Some of their most famous works of art were tombs or decorations in tombs.

> Egyptians often placed a mask over the face of a mummy to show what the person looked like.

Egyptian Religion

Religion was important to Egyptian life. Egyptians worshiped about 2,000 gods and goddesses. Each god or goddess was in charge of different things. Many of the gods had half-human and half-animal features.

Egyptians made statues of the gods and goddesses to honor them. They built temples. Egyptians also honored their gods with celebrations and gifts.

Egyptians believed that they needed to be buried with things they could use in the afterlife. Rich people built large tombs to hold these items. Kings were buried with jewelry, furniture, clothing, tools, and weapons. Many kings were even buried with full-sized boats!

Egyptians thought that a person needed his or her body in the afterlife. They made the body into a mummy so it would last a long time. They removed the body organs and put them in special jars. Then, they filled the body with salt to dry it. After 40 days, they filled the body with bags of salt or linen and resin. Resin is a sticky material that oozes from trees and plants. Finally, they wrapped the whole body in thin linen strips. They placed the jars and the mummy in a tomb.

Egyptian Art

Much of the art in ancient Egypt was religious. Artists painted on temple walls and inside tombs. Some of these pictures showed gods and goddesses. Others showed people giving offerings to the gods. Egyptian artists used earth colors in their paintings. They rarely drew a picture of a person's body from the front. Instead, they made a picture that showed the side and front of a person's body.

Much of the art also showed what daily life was like in Egypt. Some of the tomb paintings show farmers gathering barley. Others show servants bringing food or fanning their owners. Still other paintings show families eating or sitting together. They show children playing games and adults watching plays or dancing.

Sculptors carved statues out of stone. They made statues of kings, queens, gods and goddesses, and other powerful people. Some middle-class people also had statues made.

This Egyptian painting shows a mother spending time with her children.

Obelisks pointed to the sky because they were symbols of the Sun.

Egyptian Architecture

Egyptian architecture is famous. Architecture is the look and way a building is made. Egyptians were master builders. Today, many of their huge pyramids and temples are still standing, thousands of years after they were built.

Egyptians used different kinds of stone to build their large, public buildings. They carefully cut each stone block so it would fit perfectly with the blocks around it. The stones fit together like puzzle pieces. The workers started by building a foundation. A foundation is the base of a building. They made mud-brick ramps to drag the stones to the upper levels.

Kings started building their pyramid tombs as soon as they came into power. There are two kinds of Egyptian pyramids. Early pyramids were step-pyramids. Instead of being smooth, their sides looked like steps. Later pyramids had smooth sides. The largest pyramid is the smooth Great Pyramid of King Khufu at Giza. It is about 480 feet (146 m) high.

Egyptians also built stone obelisks. An obelisk is a tall, four-sided monument. The top of an Egyptian obelisk was thinner than the base and came to a point. Egyptian obelisks often had pictures carved on them.

Egyptian Cities

All of the cities in ancient Egypt were built along the Nile. People used water from the Nile to drink, bathe, and cook. They sailed from city to city. They also fished in the Nile.

Memphis was the first capital of Egypt. Memphis was built where Upper Egypt and Lower Egypt met. Memphis was about 8 miles (2.4 km) long and 4 miles (1.2 km) wide. About 50,000 people lived in Memphis. One of the king's palaces was there. Many powerful officials and priests also lived in Memphis.

A **necropolis** called Saqqara was built outside of Memphis. A necropolis is a large cemetery. Some of the first pyramids were built there.

Thebes was an important city during the New Kingdom. It was on the east bank of the Nile. A huge necropolis called Valley of the Kings and Valley of the Queens was built across from Thebes on the west bank of the Nile.

Thebes had several huge temples, including the Luxor Temple. Each temple

These are the remains of the Temple of Karnak in Thebes.

became a small city. Many smaller buildings surrounded them. There were libraries, schools, places to store grain, and buildings where priests lived.

Each year, Thebes hosted several religious celebrations to honor the gods. Important people came to Thebes for the celebrations.

These ancient Egyptian hieroglyphs are carved in the stone wall of a temple.

Writing

Egypt was one of the first civilizations to have a system of writing. The Egyptians used pictures and symbols to stand for sounds, ideas, or categories. This kind of writing is called **hieroglyphs**. Egyptians used hieroglyphs to write their history and keep records.

Egyptians wrote with brushes dipped in ocher. Ocher is an earthy yellow or red color. It is found in minerals, such as iron. Egyptians mixed ocher with glue or tree resin. They used this mixture to write.

The writing material changed over time. At first, Egyptians carved the symbols into **pottery**, clay sealings, ivory, stone, or wood. But then they found a way to make a kind of paper out of **papyrus** stalks. Papyrus is a reed plant. Egyptians wrote on the papyrus with ocher.

Papyrus was the first kind of paper. Egyptians made a lot of papyrus. They sold it to people in many different lands.

Learning

Near each temple was a center of learning called a House of Life. It was a place where people studied. Only priests or powerful men could go to a House of Life.

Priests and other men went to a House of Life to learn to read and write. They studied the stars and learned how to solve math problems. A library was one of the main features of a House of Life. There, the students could read books written on papyrus. They also wrote or copied new books to add to the library.

Poor people did not attend school. Their parents taught them the skills they needed. Children almost always stayed in the same class as their parents. They did the same job as their parents. Mothers taught daughters how to make cloth and cook. Farmers taught their sons how to farm. Merchants taught their sons how to run a business. Craftspeople taught their sons how to make shoes, jewelry, pottery, or other objects.

This is a papyrus page from an ancient Egyptian book called the *Book of the Dead*. The book is about the afterlife.

Some ancient Egyptian farming ideas are still used today. This modern irrigation ditch is like the ones used in ancient Egypt.

What Did the Egyptians Do?

Egyptian people helped shape later civilizations. Egypt formed one of the first large nation-states. A nation-state is a group of people of the same background under one government. Egyptians had a center of government and an ordered way of ruling.

Egyptian pyramids and temples have given ideas to other cultures to create their own monuments. Egyptian irrigation showed future farmers how to grow healthy crops in dry weather. Egyptians also had the first indoor bathrooms. Dirty water and waste drained through a hole in the floor.

Egyptian Discoveries

Egyptian scientists made discoveries in math and science. The modern decimal system is based on Egyptian math. The decimal system is a way of counting that is based on the number 10. Some historians believe that the Egyptians chose this number because people have 10 fingers and toes.

Egyptians also created a calendar. The Egyptian calendar was based on the movement of the Sun. It had 365 days. The days were grouped into 12 months. Each month was split into three, 10-day weeks.

Leap year was the only thing the Egyptians did not include in their calendar. Our year has 365.25 days. Each year, the Egyptian calendar lost one-fourth of a day. This amounted to one month about every 100 years.

The modern calendar is based on the Egyptian calendar. But it has a leap year. Also, weeks are 7 days instead of 10 days.

This is an Egyptian calendar stone. The symbols on it stand for groups of stars.

Egyptians also divided each day into 24 hours. But Egyptian hours were different from modern hours. They changed with the seasons. Daylight hours were longer during summer. Night hours were shorter in summer because darkness did not last 12 hours.

⬆ This is a Greek statue of Queen Cleopatra VII.
She was the last queen of Egypt.

Fall of Egypt

Foreign armies took over Egypt's land near
the end of the New Kingdom. Pharaohs led
Egyptian armies to fight the people of Libya
and the Sea Peoples. The Sea Peoples came

from islands in the Mediterranean Sea. They left their homes to find new ones.

Egyptian people grew tired of war. Pharaohs began to lose power. Priests began to gain control. The Egyptian kingdom broke into different pieces led by different people.

Rule of Egypt passed from country to country. Libyan kings ruled Egypt first. Then Nubian kings took over. Assyrians took over next and put an Egyptian governor in charge. He threw out the Assyrians and took over Egypt. After 100 years, the Persians took over Egypt. They lost Egypt when Alexander the Great of Greece made Egypt a part of Greece in 332 B.C.

Alexander's General Ptolemy took charge of Egypt when Alexander died. The Ptolemaic dynasty ruled Egypt for about 300 years. The last Ptolemaic ruler was Queen Cleopatra VII. She killed herself when the Roman army defeated Egypt in battle. Then Egypt became part of Rome.

These archaeologists are looking for artifacts in an Egyptian tomb.

We know much about Egyptian culture because other people copied the culture. Roman and Greek people used Egyptian ideas to build their own civilizations. Romans even began worshiping some Egyptian gods and goddesses.

Archaeology also shows us much about the Egyptians. Archaeology is the study of ancient remains. Archaeologists study Egyptian buildings. They carefully dig up sand-covered cities.

Archaeologists search for **artifacts**. Artifacts are objects that were made or used by humans in the past. Artifacts made by ancient Egyptians show what Egyptian life was like.

 This is the gold burial mask of King Tut. It was found in his unopened tomb.

Egyptian Sites

Some of the most exciting archaeological finds are in necropolises. Paintings cover many tomb walls. Scientists study the paintings to learn about Egyptian beliefs.

Sometimes tomb walls have stories written on them in hieroglyphs. Archaeologists study the hieroglyphs to read what they say. Some hieroglyphs tell about people's lives. Others tell about the afterlife.

Most tombs were robbed of their riches over the years. But archaeologists have found the unopened tomb of King Tutankamun, known as Tut. King Tut was a king who died young. The unopened tomb helped archaeologists learn how Egyptian kings were buried.

Archaeologists are still searching for new Egyptian sites. They think what is left of some temples, tombs, and cities are buried under sand. They hope to find new artifacts and learn more about Egyptian life.

People today continue to be interested in ancient Egypt. Each year, millions of people travel to Egypt to see the pyramids, tombs, and temples. The monuments remind people of the power and beauty of the ancient Egyptian civilization.

Glossary

archaeology (ar-kee-OL-uh-jee)—the study of ancient remains

artifact (ART-uh-fakt)—an object that was made or used by humans in the past

civilization (siv-i-luh-ZAY-shuhn)—an advanced society

class (KLASS)—a group of people in a society who have similar jobs

culture (KUHL-chur)—the way of life, ideas, customs, and traditions of a group of people

god-king (GOD-KING)—a ruler who was worshiped as a god

hieroglyphs (hye-ur-oh-GLIFSS)—a way of writing that used pictures to write words

irrigate (IHR-uh-gate)—to bring water to dry land

necropolis (ni-CRAH-poh-lis)—a huge cemetery most often found in ancient cities

papyrus (puh-PYE-ruhss)—a reed plant; also the term for a kind of paper made from the stalks of the papyrus plant

pharaoh (FAIR-oh)—the New Kingdom term for a ruler of Egypt

pottery (POT-ur-ee)—objects made of baked clay

pyramid (PIHR-uh-mid)—an ancient Egyptian stone monument where kings were buried

scribe (SKRIBE)—a person who copies books, letters, and other writing by hand

silt (SILT)—rich soil left on land after a flood

temple (TEM-puhl)—a special building used for worshiping gods

tomb (TOOM)—a grave, room, or building used for holding a dead body and burial objects

tunic (TOO-nik)—a straight, loose-fitting piece of clothing

vizier (vi-ZIR)—a king's top assistant

Internet Sites

Cyber Mummy
http://www.ncsa.uiuc.edu/Cyberia/VideoTest
    bed/Projects/Mummy/mummyhome.html

Electric Passport—Ancient Egypt
http://www.mrdowling.com/604egypt.html

Nova Online—Explore the Pyramids
http://www.pbs.org/wgbh/nova/pyramid/
    explore/

Tour Egypt
http://touregypt.net/kids

Useful Addresses

Institute of Egyptian Art & Archaeology
Communication and Fine Arts Building
Room 142
University of Memphis
3750 Norriswood Avenue
Memphis, TN 38152

The Oriental Institute Museum
1155 East 58th Street
Chicago, IL 60637

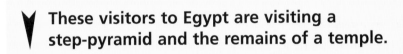

▼ These visitors to Egypt are visiting a step-pyramid and the remains of a temple.

Index